Syncopation Rules!

Five Later Elementary Level Piano Solos
by
Carolyn Miller

Contents

12141

Happy Go Lucky

(Rag)

Carolyn Miller

f
mf
f
mf

mf
f

Marumba

Joyfully ♩= 138

Carolyn Miller

mf
f

mp
f
mp
mf
f
8vb

Ragtime in F

Moderato ♩ = 135-145

Carolyn Miller

crescendo
mf
mp

Westward Bound

Moderato ♩= 135

Carolyn Miller

mp

f
2
mp
rit.
8vb

The Rain Dance

With energy ♩ = 105

Carolyn Miller

1
mp
1 2 1
mf

ff
8va